Multiplication
Numbers 1 to 10

KUMON

Multiplication: 2

date / / score /100

1 Trace or write the missing numbers. 5 points per question

①
1	2	3	4	5	6	7	8	9	10
11	12	13	14	15	16	17	18	19	20

②
2	4	6	8	10	12	14	16	18	20

③
2	4	6	8	10	12	14	16	18	20

④
2	4	6	8	10	12	14	16	18	20

2 Trace the answer in the number sentence. 2 points per question

① $2 \times 1 = 2$

② $2 \times 2 = 4$

③ $2 \times 3 = 6$

④ $2 \times 4 = 8$

⑤ $2 \times 5 = 10$

⑥ $2 \times 6 = 12$

⑦ $2 \times 7 = 14$

⑧ $2 \times 8 = 16$

⑨ $2 \times 9 = 18$

⑩ $2 \times 10 = 20$

3 Multiply.

3 points per question

① 2 × 1 = 2

② 2 × 2 = 4

③ 2 × 3 = 6

④ 2 × 4 = 8

⑤ 2 × 5 = 10

⑥ 2 × 6 = 12

⑦ 2 × 7 = 14

⑧ 2 × 8 = 16

⑨ 2 × 9 = 18

⑩ 2 × 10 = 20

4 Multiply.

3 points per question

① 2 × 1 = 2

② 2 × 2 = 4

③ 2 × 3 = 6

④ 2 × 4 = 8

⑤ 2 × 5 = 10

⑥ 2 × 6 = 12

⑦ 2 × 7 = 14

⑧ 2 × 8 = 16

⑨ 2 × 9 = 18

⑩ 2 × 10 = 20

2 Multiplication: 2

1 Multiply.

2 points per question

① $2 \times 1 = 2$

② $2 \times 2 = 4$

③ $2 \times 3 = 6$

④ $2 \times 4 = 8$

⑤ $2 \times 5 = 10$

⑥ $2 \times 6 = 12$

⑦ $2 \times 7 = 14$

⑧ $2 \times 8 = 16$

⑨ $2 \times 9 = 18$

⑩ $2 \times 10 = 20$

2 Multiply.

2 points per question

① $2 \times 3 = 6$

② $2 \times 10 = 20$

③ $2 \times 5 = 10$

④ $2 \times 2 = 4$

⑤ $2 \times 4 = 8$

⑥ $2 \times 1 = 2$

⑦ $2 \times 9 = 18$

⑧ $2 \times 7 = 14$

⑨ $2 \times 6 = 12$

⑩ $2 \times 8 = 16$

3 Multiply.

3 points per question

① 2 × 3 = 6

② 2 × 9 = 18

③ 2 × 10 = 20

④ 2 × 1 = 2

⑤ 2 × 5 = 10

⑥ 2 × 2 = 4

⑦ 2 × 7 = 14

⑧ 2 × 4 = 8

⑨ 2 × 8 = 16

⑩ 2 × 1 = 2

⑪ 2 × 6 = 12

⑫ 2 × 3 = 6

⑬ 2 × 7 = 14

⑭ 2 × 10 = 20

⑮ 2 × 4 = 8

⑯ 2 × 6 = 12

⑰ 2 × 9 = 18

⑱ 2 × 2 = 4

⑲ 2 × 8 = 16

⑳ 2 × 5 = 10

Keep going. Your work will pay off.

3 Multiplication: 3

date / / score /100

1 Trace or write the missing numbers. (5 points per question)

1	2	3	4	5	6	7	8	9	10
① 11	12	13	14	15	16	17	18	19	20
21	22	23	24	25	26	27	28	29	30

②	3	6	9	12	15	18	21	24	27	30

③	3	6	9	12	15	18	21	24	27	30

④	3	6	9	12	15	18	21	24	27	30

2 Trace the answer in the number sentence. (2 points per question)

① 3 × 1 = 3   ⑥ 3 × 6 = 18

② 3 × 2 = 6   ⑦ 3 × 7 = 21

③ 3 × 3 = 9   ⑧ 3 × 8 = 24

④ 3 × 4 = 12   ⑨ 3 × 9 = 27

⑤ 3 × 5 = 15   ⑩ 3 × 10 = 30

3 Multiply.

3 points per question

① $3 \times 1 = 3$

② $3 \times 2 = 6$

③ $3 \times 3 = 9$

④ $3 \times 4 = 12$

⑤ $3 \times 5 = 15$

⑥ $3 \times 6 = 18$

⑦ $3 \times 7 = 21$

⑧ $3 \times 8 = 24$

⑨ $3 \times 9 = 27$

⑩ $3 \times 10 = 30$

4 Multiply.

3 points per question

① $3 \times 1 = 3$

② $3 \times 2 = 6$

③ $3 \times 3 = 9$

④ $3 \times 4 = 12$

⑤ $3 \times 5 = 15$

⑥ $3 \times 6 = 18$

⑦ $3 \times 7 = 21$

⑧ $3 \times 8 = 24$

⑨ $3 \times 9 = 27$

⑩ $3 \times 10 = 30$

date / / score /100

1 Multiply.

2 points per question

① $3 \times 1 = 3$

② $3 \times 2 = 6$

③ $3 \times 3 = 9$

④ $3 \times 4 = 12$

⑤ $3 \times 5 = 15$

⑥ $3 \times 6 = 18$

⑦ $3 \times 7 = 21$

⑧ $3 \times 8 = 24$

⑨ $3 \times 9 = 27$

⑩ $3 \times 10 = 30$

2 Multiply.

2 points per question

① $3 \times 8 = 24$

② $3 \times 7 = 21$

③ $3 \times 1 = 3$

④ $3 \times 2 = 6$

⑤ $3 \times 10 = 30$

⑥ $3 \times 6 = 18$

⑦ $3 \times 9 = 27$

⑧ $3 \times 4 = 12$

⑨ $3 \times 5 = 15$

⑩ $3 \times 3 = 9$

3 Multiply.

3 points per question

① 3 × 5 = 15

② 3 × 8 = 16

③ 3 × 2 = 6

④ 3 × 9 = 27

⑤ 3 × 6 = 18

⑥ 3 × 4 = 12

⑦ 3 × 10 = 30

⑧ 3 × 7 = 14

⑨ 3 × 3 = 9

⑩ 3 × 6 = 18

⑪ 3 × 1 = 3

⑫ 3 × 8 = 16

⑬ 3 × 4 = 12

⑭ 3 × 7 = 21

⑮ 3 × 2 = 6

⑯ 3 × 5 = 15

⑰ 3 × 1 = 3

⑱ 3 × 10 = 30

⑲ 3 × 9 = 27

⑳ 3 × 3 = 9

Good job!

1 Multiply.
2 points per question

① $2 \times 1 = 2$

② $2 \times 2 = 4$

③ $2 \times 3 = 6$

④ $2 \times 4 = 8$

⑤ $2 \times 5 = 10$

⑥ $2 \times 6 = 12$

⑦ $2 \times 7 = 14$

⑧ $2 \times 8 = 16$

⑨ $2 \times 9 = 18$

⑩ $2 \times 10 = 20$

2 Multiply.
2 points per question

① $3 \times 1 = 3$

② $3 \times 2 = 6$

③ $3 \times 3 = 9$

④ $3 \times 4 = 12$

⑤ $3 \times 5 = 15$

⑥ $3 \times 6 = 18$

⑦ $3 \times 7 = 21$

⑧ $3 \times 8 = 24$

⑨ $3 \times 9 = 27$

⑩ $3 \times 10 = 30$

3 Multiply.

3 points per question

① 2 × 5 = 10

② 3 × 8 = 24

③ 2 × 2 = 4

④ 2 × 9 = 18

⑤ 3 × 6 = 18

⑥ 3 × 4 = 12

⑦ 2 × 10 = 20

⑧ 3 × 7 = 21

⑨ 2 × 3 = 6

⑩ 2 × 6 = 12

⑪ 3 × 1 = 3

⑫ 2 × 8 = 16

⑬ 2 × 4 = 8

⑭ 2 × 7 = 14

⑮ 3 × 2 = 6

⑯ 3 × 5 = 15

⑰ 2 × 1 = 2

⑱ 3 × 10 = 30

⑲ 3 × 9 = 27

⑳ 3 × 3 = 9

You're doing great!

6 Multiplication: 4

date   /   /   score   /100

1 Trace or write the missing numbers.

5 points per question

①
1	2	3	4	5	6	7	8	9	10
11	12	13	14	15	16	17	18	19	20
21	22	23	24	25	26	27	28	29	30
31	32	33	34	35	36	37	38	39	40

②
4	8	12	16	20	24	28	32	36	40

③
4	8	12	16	20	24	28	32	36	40

④
4	8	12	16	20	24	28	32	36	40

2 Trace the answer in the number sentence.

2 points per question

① $4 \times 1 = 4$

② $4 \times 2 = 8$

③ $4 \times 3 = 12$

④ $4 \times 4 = 16$

⑤ $4 \times 5 = 20$

⑥ $4 \times 6 = 24$

⑦ $4 \times 7 = 28$

⑧ $4 \times 8 = 32$

⑨ $4 \times 9 = 36$

⑩ $4 \times 10 = 40$

3 Multiply.

3 points per question

① 4 × 1 = 4

② 4 × 2 = 8

③ 4 × 3 = 12

④ 4 × 4 = 16

⑤ 4 × 5 = 20

⑥ 4 × 6 = 24

⑦ 4 × 7 = 28

⑧ 4 × 8 = 32

⑨ 4 × 9 = 36

⑩ 4 × 10 = 40

4 Multiply.

3 points per question

① 4 × 1 = 4

② 4 × 2 = 8

③ 4 × 3 = 12

④ 4 × 4 = 16

⑤ 4 × 5 = 20

⑥ 4 × 6 = 24

⑦ 4 × 7 = 28

⑧ 4 × 8 = 32

⑨ 4 × 9 = 36

⑩ 4 × 10 = 40

7 Multiplication: 4

date / / score /100

1 Multiply.

(2 points per question)

① $4 \times 1 = 4$

② $4 \times 2 = 8$

③ $4 \times 3 = 12$

④ $4 \times 4 = 16$

⑤ $4 \times 5 = 20$

⑥ $4 \times 6 = 24$

⑦ $4 \times 7 = 28$

⑧ $4 \times 8 = 32$

⑨ $4 \times 9 = 36$

⑩ $4 \times 10 = 40$

2 Multiply.

(2 points per question)

① $4 \times 3 = 12$

② $4 \times 7 = 28$

③ $4 \times 4 = 16$

④ $4 \times 2 = 8$

⑤ $4 \times 9 = 36$

⑥ $4 \times 6 = 24$

⑦ $4 \times 10 = 40$

⑧ $4 \times 8 = 32$

⑨ $4 \times 1 = 4$

⑩ $4 \times 5 = 20$

3 Multiply.

(3 points per question)

① 4 × 9 = 36

② 4 × 3 = 12

③ 4 × 1 = 4

④ 4 × 10 = 40

⑤ 4 × 2 = 8

⑥ 4 × 5 = 20

⑦ 4 × 7 = 28

⑧ 4 × 4 = 16

⑨ 4 × 8 = 32

⑩ 4 × 6 = 24

⑪ 4 × 1 = 4

⑫ 4 × 7 = 28

⑬ 4 × 3 = 12

⑭ 4 × 10 = 40

⑮ 4 × 6 = 24

⑯ 4 × 4 = 16

⑰ 4 × 2 = 8

⑱ 4 × 9 = 36

⑲ 4 × 5 = 20

⑳ 4 × 8 = 32

Keep up the good work!

8 Multiplication: 5

1 Trace or write the missing numbers.

5 points per question

①

1	2	3	4	5	6	7	8	9	10
11	12	13	14	15	16	17	18	19	20
21	22	23	24	25	26	27	28	29	30
31	32	33	34	35	36	37	38	39	40

② | 5 | 10 | 15 | 20 | 25 | 30 | 35 | 40 | 45 | 50 |

③ | 5 | 10 | 15 | 20 | 25 | 30 | 35 | 40 | 45 | 50 |

④ | 5 | 10 | 15 | 20 | 25 | 30 | 35 | 40 | 45 | 50 |

2 Trace the answer in the number sentence.

2 points per question

① $5 \times 1 = 5$

② $5 \times 2 = 10$

③ $5 \times 3 = 15$

④ $5 \times 4 = 20$

⑤ $5 \times 5 = 25$

⑥ $5 \times 6 = 30$

⑦ $5 \times 7 = 35$

⑧ $5 \times 8 = 40$

⑨ $5 \times 9 = 45$

⑩ $5 \times 10 = 50$

3 Multiply.

3 points per question

① $5 \times 1 = 5$

② $5 \times 2 = 10$

③ $5 \times 3 = 15$

④ $5 \times 4 = 20$

⑤ $5 \times 5 = 25$

⑥ $5 \times 6 = 30$

⑦ $5 \times 7 = 35$

⑧ $5 \times 8 = 40$

⑨ $5 \times 9 = 45$

⑩ $5 \times 10 = 50$

4 Multiply.

3 points per question

① $5 \times 1 = 5$

② $5 \times 2 = 10$

③ $5 \times 3 = 15$

④ $5 \times 4 = 20$

⑤ $5 \times 5 = 25$

⑥ $5 \times 6 = 30$

⑦ $5 \times 7 = 35$

⑧ $5 \times 8 = 40$

⑨ $5 \times 9 = 45$

⑩ $5 \times 10 = 50$

date / / score /100

1 Multiply.   2 points per question

① $5 \times 1 = 5$ ⑥ $5 \times 6 = 30$

② $5 \times 2 = 10$ ⑦ $5 \times 7 = 35$

③ $5 \times 3 = 15$ ⑧ $5 \times 8 = 40$

④ $5 \times 4 = 20$ ⑨ $5 \times 9 = 45$

⑤ $5 \times 5 = 25$ ⑩ $5 \times 10 = 50$

2 Multiply.   2 points per question

① $5 \times 5 = 25$ ⑥ $5 \times 9 = 45$

② $5 \times 1 = 5$ ⑦ $5 \times 2 = 10$

③ $5 \times 8 = 40$ ⑧ $5 \times 4 = 20$

④ $5 \times 10 = 50$ ⑨ $5 \times 7 = 35$

⑤ $5 \times 6 = 30$ ⑩ $5 \times 3 = 15$

3 Multiply.

3 points per question

① $5 \times 8 = 40$

② $5 \times 5 = 25$

③ $5 \times 9 = 45$

④ $5 \times 2 = 10$

⑤ $5 \times 4 = 20$

⑥ $5 \times 6 = 30$

⑦ $5 \times 10 = 50$

⑧ $5 \times 3 = 15$

⑨ $5 \times 7 = 35$

⑩ $5 \times 1 = 5$

⑪ $5 \times 6 = 30$

⑫ $5 \times 8 = 40$

⑬ $5 \times 4 = 20$

⑭ $5 \times 7 = 35$

⑮ $5 \times 5 = 25$

⑯ $5 \times 2 = 10$

⑰ $5 \times 10 = 50$

⑱ $5 \times 1 = 5$

⑲ $5 \times 3 = 15$

⑳ $5 \times 9 = 45$

What wonderful work!

1 Multiply.

2 points per question

① $4 \times 1 = 4$

② $4 \times 2 = 8$

③ $4 \times 3 = 12$

④ $4 \times 4 = 16$

⑤ $4 \times 5 = 20$

⑥ $4 \times 6 = 24$

⑦ $4 \times 7 = 28$

⑧ $4 \times 8 = 32$

⑨ $4 \times 9 = 36$

⑩ $4 \times 10 = 40$

2 Multiply.

2 points per question

① $5 \times 1 = 5$

② $5 \times 2 = 10$

③ $5 \times 3 = 15$

④ $5 \times 4 = 20$

⑤ $5 \times 5 = 25$

⑥ $5 \times 6 = 30$

⑦ $5 \times 7 = 35$

⑧ $5 \times 8 = 40$

⑨ $5 \times 9 = 45$

⑩ $5 \times 10 = 50$

3 Multiply.

① $3 \times 3 = 9$

② $4 \times 8 = 32$

③ $5 \times 2 = 10$

④ $3 \times 5 = 15$

⑤ $2 \times 8 = 16$

⑥ $2 \times 9 = 18$

⑦ $4 \times 10 = 40$

⑧ $5 \times 7 = 35$

⑨ $3 \times 8 = 24$

⑩ $4 \times 6 = 24$

⑪ $2 \times 6 = 12$

⑫ $5 \times 8 = 40$

⑬ $3 \times 7 = 21$

⑭ $3 \times 2 = 6$

⑮ $4 \times 2 = 8$

⑯ $4 \times 5 = 20$

⑰ $2 \times 10 = 20$

⑱ $2 \times 2 = 4$

⑲ $5 \times 9 = 45$

⑳ $4 \times 3 = 12$

You should be very proud!

Multiplication: 6

date   /   /   score   /100

1 Trace or write the missing numbers.   (5 points per question)

①

1	2	3	4	5	6	7	8	9	10
11	12	13	14	15	16	17	18	19	20
21	22	23	24	25	26	27	28	29	30
31	32	33	34	35	36	37	38	39	40

②

6	12	18	24	30	36	42	48	54	60

③

6	12	18	24	30	36	42	48	54	60

④

6	12	18	24	30	36	42	48	54	60

2 Trace the answer in the number sentence.   (2 points per question)

① $6 \times 1 = 6$

② $6 \times 2 = 12$

③ $6 \times 3 = 18$

④ $6 \times 4 = 24$

⑤ $6 \times 5 = 30$

⑥ $6 \times 6 = 36$

⑦ $6 \times 7 = 42$

⑧ $6 \times 8 = 48$

⑨ $6 \times 9 = 54$

⑩ $6 \times 10 = 60$

3 Multiply.

3 points per question

① $6 \times 1 = 6$

② $6 \times 2 = 12$

③ $6 \times 3 = 18$

④ $6 \times 4 = 24$

⑤ $6 \times 5 = 30$

⑥ $6 \times 6 = 36$

⑦ $6 \times 7 = 42$

⑧ $6 \times 8 = 48$

⑨ $6 \times 9 = 54$

⑩ $6 \times 10 = 60$

4 Multiply.

3 points per question

① $6 \times 1 = 6$

② $6 \times 2 = 12$

③ $6 \times 3 = 18$

④ $6 \times 4 = 24$

⑤ $6 \times 5 = 30$

⑥ $6 \times 6 = 36$

⑦ $6 \times 7 = 42$

⑧ $6 \times 8 = 48$

⑨ $6 \times 9 = 54$

⑩ $6 \times 10 = 60$

date   /   /   score   /100

1 Multiply.

2 points per question

① $6 \times 1 = 6$

② $6 \times 2 = 12$

③ $6 \times 3 = 18$

④ $6 \times 4 = 24$

⑤ $6 \times 5 = 30$

⑥ $6 \times 6 = 36$

⑦ $6 \times 7 = 42$

⑧ $6 \times 8 = 48$

⑨ $6 \times 9 = 54$

⑩ $6 \times 10 = 60$

2 Multiply.

2 points per question

① $6 \times 7 = 42$

② $6 \times 2 = 12$

③ $6 \times 6 = 36$

④ $6 \times 1 = 6$

⑤ $6 \times 5 = 30$

⑥ $6 \times 9 = 54$

⑦ $6 \times 4 = 24$

⑧ $6 \times 8 = 48$

⑨ $6 \times 3 = 18$

⑩ $6 \times 10 = 60$

3 Multiply.

① $6 \times 3 = 18$

② $6 \times 9 = 54$

③ $6 \times 1 = 6$

④ $6 \times 10 = 60$

⑤ $6 \times 5 = 30$

⑥ $6 \times 2 = 12$

⑦ $6 \times 4 = 24$

⑧ $6 \times 7 = 42$

⑨ $6 \times 6 = 36$

⑩ $6 \times 8 = 48$

⑪ $6 \times 7 = 42$

⑫ $6 \times 1 = 6$

⑬ $6 \times 3 = 18$

⑭ $6 \times 6 = 36$

⑮ $6 \times 10 = 60$

⑯ $6 \times 2 = 12$

⑰ $6 \times 5 = 30$

⑱ $6 \times 9 = 54$

⑲ $6 \times 4 = 24$

⑳ $6 \times 8 = 48$

You are clever!

Multiplication: 7

date / /   score /100

1 Trace or write the missing numbers. [5 points per question]

①

1	2	3	4	5	6	7	8	9	10
11	12	13	14	15	16	17	18	19	20
21	22	23	24	25	26	27	28	29	30
31	32	33	34	35	36	37	38	39	40

②

7	14	21	28	35	42	49	56	63	70

③

	14		28		42		56		70

④

7		21	28	35				63	

2 Trace the answer in the number sentence. [2 points per question]

① $7 \times 1 = 7$

② $7 \times 2 = 14$

③ $7 \times 3 = 21$

④ $7 \times 4 = 28$

⑤ $7 \times 5 = 35$

⑥ $7 \times 6 = 42$

⑦ $7 \times 7 = 49$

⑧ $7 \times 8 = 56$

⑨ $7 \times 9 = 63$

⑩ $7 \times 10 = 70$

3 Multiply.

① $7 \times 1 = 7$

② $7 \times 2 = 14$

③ $7 \times 3 =$

④ $7 \times 4 = 28$

⑤ $7 \times 5 =$

⑥ $7 \times 6 =$

⑦ $7 \times 7 =$

⑧ $7 \times 8 = 56$

⑨ $7 \times 9 =$

⑩ $7 \times 10 =$

4 Multiply.

① $7 \times 1 =$

② $7 \times 2 =$

③ $7 \times 3 =$

④ $7 \times 4 =$

⑤ $7 \times 5 =$

⑥ $7 \times 6 =$

⑦ $7 \times 7 =$

⑧ $7 \times 8 =$

⑨ $7 \times 9 =$

⑩ $7 \times 10 =$

date / / score /100

1 Multiply.

2 points per question

① $7 \times 1 =$

② $7 \times 2 =$

③ $7 \times 3 =$

④ $7 \times 4 =$

⑤ $7 \times 5 =$

⑥ $7 \times 6 =$

⑦ $7 \times 7 =$

⑧ $7 \times 8 =$

⑨ $7 \times 9 =$

⑩ $7 \times 10 =$

2 Multiply.

2 points per question

① $7 \times 3 =$

② $7 \times 8 =$

③ $7 \times 10 =$

④ $7 \times 4 =$

⑤ $7 \times 9 =$

⑥ $7 \times 5 =$

⑦ $7 \times 6 =$

⑧ $7 \times 2 =$

⑨ $7 \times 1 =$

⑩ $7 \times 7 =$

3 Multiply.

3 points per question

① $7 \times 4 =$

② $7 \times 8 =$

③ $7 \times 2 =$

④ $7 \times 5 =$

⑤ $7 \times 9 =$

⑥ $7 \times 6 =$

⑦ $7 \times 10 =$

⑧ $7 \times 3 =$

⑨ $7 \times 1 =$

⑩ $7 \times 8 =$

⑪ $7 \times 7 =$

⑫ $7 \times 2 =$

⑬ $7 \times 6 =$

⑭ $7 \times 4 =$

⑮ $7 \times 7 =$

⑯ $7 \times 10 =$

⑰ $7 \times 1 =$

⑱ $7 \times 5 =$

⑲ $7 \times 3 =$

⑳ $7 \times 9 =$

Keep it up. You're doing great.

1 Multiply. 2 points per question

① 6 × 1 =

② 6 × 2 =

③ 6 × 3 =

④ 6 × 4 =

⑤ 6 × 5 =

⑥ 6 × 6 =

⑦ 6 × 7 =

⑧ 6 × 8 =

⑨ 6 × 9 =

⑩ 6 × 10 =

2 Multiply. 2 points per question

① 7 × 1 =

② 7 × 2 =

③ 7 × 3 =

④ 7 × 4 =

⑤ 7 × 5 =

⑥ 7 × 6 =

⑦ 7 × 7 =

⑧ 7 × 8 =

⑨ 7 × 9 =

⑩ 7 × 10 =

3 Multiply.

3 points per question

① 3 × 5 =

② 5 × 8 =

③ 4 × 2 =

④ 2 × 9 =

⑤ 6 × 6 =

⑥ 7 × 4 =

⑦ 2 × 10 =

⑧ 6 × 7 =

⑨ 3 × 3 =

⑩ 5 × 6 =

⑪ 7 × 1 =

⑫ 4 × 8 =

⑬ 3 × 4 =

⑭ 7 × 7 =

⑮ 2 × 2 =

⑯ 4 × 5 =

⑰ 5 × 1 =

⑱ 6 × 10 =

⑲ 7 × 9 =

⑳ 6 × 3 =

Good job!

16 Multiplication: 8

1 Trace or write the missing numbers. (5 points per question)

①

1	2	3	4	5	6	7	8	9	10
11	12	13	14	15	16	17	18	19	20
21	22	23	24	25	26	27	28	29	30
31	32	33	34	35	36	37	38	39	40

② | 8 | 16 | 24 | 32 | 40 | 48 | 56 | 64 | 72 | 80 |

③ | 8 | 16 | 24 | 32 | 40 | 48 | 56 | 64 | 72 | 80 |

④ | 8 | 16 | 24 | 32 | 40 | 48 | 56 | 64 | 72 | 80 |

2 Trace the answer in the number sentence. (2 points per question)

① 8 × 1 = 8

② 8 × 2 = 16

③ 8 × 3 = 24

④ 8 × 4 = 32

⑤ 8 × 5 = 40

⑥ 8 × 6 = 48

⑦ 8 × 7 = 56

⑧ 8 × 8 = 64

⑨ 8 × 9 = 72

⑩ 8 × 10 = 80

©Kumon Publishing Co., Ltd.

3 Multiply.

3 points per question

① 8 × 1 = 8

② 8 × 2 = 16

③ 8 × 3 = 24

④ 8 × 4 = 32

⑤ 8 × 5 = 40

⑥ 8 × 6 = 48

⑦ 8 × 7 = 56

⑧ 8 × 8 = 64

⑨ 8 × 9 = 72

⑩ 8 × 10 = 80

4 Multiply.

3 points per question

① 8 × 1 = 8

② 8 × 2 = 16

③ 8 × 3 = 24

④ 8 × 4 = 32

⑤ 8 × 5 = 40

⑥ 8 × 6 = 48

⑦ 8 × 7 = 56

⑧ 8 × 8 = 64

⑨ 8 × 9 = 72

⑩ 8 × 10 = 80

date / / score /100

1 Multiply.

2 points per question

① $8 \times 1 = 8$

② $8 \times 2 = 16$

③ $8 \times 3 = 24$

④ $8 \times 4 = 32$

⑤ $8 \times 5 = 40$

⑥ $8 \times 6 = 48$

⑦ $8 \times 7 = 56$

⑧ $8 \times 8 = 64$

⑨ $8 \times 9 = 72$

⑩ $8 \times 10 = 80$

2 Multiply.

2 points per question

① $8 \times 7 = 56$

② $8 \times 2 = 16$

③ $8 \times 6 = 48$

④ $8 \times 1 = 8$

⑤ $8 \times 9 = 72$

⑥ $8 \times 5 = 40$

⑦ $8 \times 10 = 80$

⑧ $8 \times 4 = 32$

⑨ $8 \times 8 = 64$

⑩ $8 \times 3 = 24$

3 Multiply.

3 points per question

① $8 \times 3 = 24$

② $8 \times 9 = 72$

③ $8 \times 5 = 40$

④ $8 \times 1 = 8$

⑤ $8 \times 10 = 60$

⑥ $8 \times 7 = 56$

⑦ $8 \times 4 = 32$

⑧ $8 \times 6 = 48$

⑨ $8 \times 2 = 16$

⑩ $8 \times 7 = 56$

⑪ $8 \times 8 = 64$

⑫ $8 \times 1 = 8$

⑬ $8 \times 3 = 24$

⑭ $8 \times 10 = 8$

⑮ $8 \times 6 = 48$

⑯ $8 \times 9 = 72$

⑰ $8 \times 5 = 4$

⑱ $8 \times 2 = 16$

⑲ $8 \times 8 = 64$

⑳ $8 \times 4 = 32$

You're a star!

date / / score /100

1 Trace or write the missing numbers. (5 points per question)

①

1	2	3	4	5	6	7	8	9	10
11	12	13	14	15	16	17	18	19	20
21	22	23	24	25	26	27	28	29	30
31	32	33	34	35	36	37	38	39	40

②

9	18	27	36	45	54	63	72	81	90

③

	18		36		54		72		90

④

9				45	54		72	81	

2 Trace the answer in the number sentence. (2 points per question)

① $9 \times 1 = 9$

② $9 \times 2 = 18$

③ $9 \times 3 = 27$

④ $9 \times 4 = 36$

⑤ $9 \times 5 = 45$

⑥ $9 \times 6 = 54$

⑦ $9 \times 7 = 63$

⑧ $9 \times 8 = 72$

⑨ $9 \times 9 = 81$

⑩ $9 \times 10 = 90$

3 Multiply.

3 points per question

① $9 \times 1 = 9$

② $9 \times 2 = 18$

③ $9 \times 3 =$

④ $9 \times 4 = 36$

⑤ $9 \times 5 =$

⑥ $9 \times 6 =$

⑦ $9 \times 7 = 63$

⑧ $9 \times 8 =$

⑨ $9 \times 9 =$

⑩ $9 \times 10 =$

4 Multiply.

3 points per question

① $9 \times 1 =$

② $9 \times 2 =$

③ $9 \times 3 =$

④ $9 \times 4 =$

⑤ $9 \times 5 =$

⑥ $9 \times 6 =$

⑦ $9 \times 7 =$

⑧ $9 \times 8 =$

⑨ $9 \times 9 =$

⑩ $9 \times 10 =$

19 Multiplication: 9

date   /   /   score   /100

1 Multiply.

2 points per question

① 9 × 1 = 9

② 9 × 2 = 18

③ 9 × 3 = 27

④ 9 × 4 = 36

⑤ 9 × 5 = 45

⑥ 9 × 6 = 54

⑦ 9 × 7 = 63

⑧ 9 × 8 = 72

⑨ 9 × 9 = 81

⑩ 9 × 10 = 90

2 Multiply.

2 points per question

① 9 × 8 = 72

② 9 × 4 = 36

③ 9 × 10 = 90

④ 9 × 5 = 45

⑤ 9 × 3 = 27

⑥ 9 × 1 = 9

⑦ 9 × 6 = 54

⑧ 9 × 2 = 18

⑨ 9 × 7 = 63

⑩ 9 × 9 = 81

38 ©Kumon Publishing Co., Ltd.

3 Multiply.

3 points per question

① $9 \times 4 = 36$

② $9 \times 2 = 18$

③ $9 \times 8 =$

④ $9 \times 5 =$

⑤ $9 \times 9 =$

⑥ $9 \times 6 =$

⑦ $9 \times 3 =$

⑧ $9 \times 10 =$

⑨ $9 \times 1 =$

⑩ $9 \times 8 =$

⑪ $9 \times 2 =$

⑫ $9 \times 7 =$

⑬ $9 \times 4 =$

⑭ $9 \times 6 =$

⑮ $9 \times 10 =$

⑯ $9 \times 5 =$

⑰ $9 \times 9 =$

⑱ $9 \times 1 =$

⑲ $9 \times 7 =$

⑳ $9 \times 3 =$

Excellent!

1 Multiply.
2 points per question

① $8 \times 1 =$

② $8 \times 2 =$

③ $8 \times 3 =$

④ $8 \times 4 =$

⑤ $8 \times 5 =$

⑥ $8 \times 6 =$

⑦ $8 \times 7 =$

⑧ $8 \times 8 =$

⑨ $8 \times 9 =$

⑩ $8 \times 10 =$

2 Multiply.
2 points per question

① $9 \times 1 =$

② $9 \times 2 =$

③ $9 \times 3 =$

④ $9 \times 4 =$

⑤ $9 \times 5 =$

⑥ $9 \times 6 =$

⑦ $9 \times 7 =$

⑧ $9 \times 8 =$

⑨ $9 \times 9 =$

⑩ $9 \times 10 =$

3 Multiply.

3 points per question

① 8 × 1 =

② 9 × 8 =

③ 2 × 4 =

④ 4 × 7 =

⑤ 5 × 2 =

⑥ 3 × 5 =

⑦ 6 × 1 =

⑧ 7 × 10 =

⑨ 2 × 9 =

⑩ 8 × 3 =

⑪ 7 × 5 =

⑫ 4 × 8 =

⑬ 9 × 2 =

⑭ 3 × 9 =

⑮ 5 × 6 =

⑯ 6 × 4 =

⑰ 8 × 10 =

⑱ 9 × 7 =

⑲ 7 × 3 =

⑳ 6 × 6 =

Well done!

Multiplication: 10

date / / score /100

1 Trace or write the missing numbers. [5 points per question]

①

1	2	3	4	5	6	7	8	9	10
11	12	13	14	15	16	17	18	19	20
21	22	23	24	25	26	27	28	29	30
31	32	33	34	35	36	37	38	39	40

②

10	20	30	40	50	60	70	80	90	100

③

10		30		50		70		90	

④

	20		40	50			80		100

2 Trace the answer in the number sentence. [2 points per question]

① $10 \times 1 = 10$

② $10 \times 2 = 20$

③ $10 \times 3 = 30$

④ $10 \times 4 = 40$

⑤ $10 \times 5 = 50$

⑥ $10 \times 6 = 60$

⑦ $10 \times 7 = 70$

⑧ $10 \times 8 = 80$

⑨ $10 \times 9 = 90$

⑩ $10 \times 10 = 100$

3 Multiply.

① $10 \times 1 = 10$

② $10 \times 2 =$

③ $10 \times 3 =$

④ $10 \times 4 =$

⑤ $10 \times 5 =$

⑥ $10 \times 6 =$

⑦ $10 \times 7 =$

⑧ $10 \times 8 =$

⑨ $10 \times 9 =$

⑩ $10 \times 10 = 100$

4 Multiply.

① $10 \times 1 =$

② $10 \times 2 =$

③ $10 \times 3 =$

④ $10 \times 4 =$

⑤ $10 \times 5 =$

⑥ $10 \times 6 =$

⑦ $10 \times 7 =$

⑧ $10 \times 8 =$

⑨ $10 \times 9 =$

⑩ $10 \times 10 =$

date / / score /100

1 Multiply.

2 points per question

① $10 \times 1 =$

② $10 \times 2 =$

③ $10 \times 3 =$

④ $10 \times 4 =$

⑤ $10 \times 5 =$

⑥ $10 \times 6 =$

⑦ $10 \times 7 =$

⑧ $10 \times 8 =$

⑨ $10 \times 9 =$

⑩ $10 \times 10 =$

2 Multiply.

2 points per question

① $10 \times 9 =$

② $10 \times 7 =$

③ $10 \times 2 =$

④ $10 \times 6 =$

⑤ $10 \times 1 =$

⑥ $10 \times 3 =$

⑦ $10 \times 5 =$

⑧ $10 \times 10 =$

⑨ $10 \times 4 =$

⑩ $10 \times 8 =$

3 Multiply.

① $10 \times 8 =$

② $10 \times 1 =$

③ $10 \times 10 =$

④ $10 \times 3 =$

⑤ $10 \times 6 =$

⑥ $10 \times 9 =$

⑦ $10 \times 5 =$

⑧ $10 \times 8 =$

⑨ $10 \times 2 =$

⑩ $10 \times 4 =$

⑪ $10 \times 3 =$

⑫ $10 \times 7 =$

⑬ $10 \times 1 =$

⑭ $10 \times 9 =$

⑮ $10 \times 5 =$

⑯ $10 \times 10 =$

⑰ $10 \times 6 =$

⑱ $10 \times 4 =$

⑲ $10 \times 7 =$

⑳ $10 \times 2 =$

Wow! You did it!

date / / score /100

1 Trace or write the missing numbers. (5 points per question)

① | 1 | 2 | 3 | 4 | 5 | 6 | 7 | 8 | 9 | 10 |

② | 1 | | 3 | | 5 | | 7 | | 9 | |

③ | 1 | 2 | | 4 | | 6 | | 8 | | 10 |

④ | 1 | | | | 5 | | | | | 10 |

2 Trace the answer in the number sentence. (2 points per question)

① $1 \times 1 = 1$

② $1 \times 2 = 2$

③ $1 \times 3 = 3$

④ $1 \times 4 = 4$

⑤ $1 \times 5 = 5$

⑥ $1 \times 6 = 6$

⑦ $1 \times 7 = 7$

⑧ $1 \times 8 = 8$

⑨ $1 \times 9 = 9$

⑩ $1 \times 10 = 10$

3 Multiply. 3 points per question

① $1 \times 1 = 1$

② $1 \times 2 = 2$

③ $1 \times 3 =$

④ $1 \times 4 =$

⑤ $1 \times 5 =$

⑥ $1 \times 6 =$

⑦ $1 \times 7 =$

⑧ $1 \times 8 =$

⑨ $1 \times 9 =$

⑩ $1 \times 10 = 10$

4 Multiply. 3 points per question

① $1 \times 1 =$

② $1 \times 2 =$

③ $1 \times 3 =$

④ $1 \times 4 =$

⑤ $1 \times 5 =$

⑥ $1 \times 6 =$

⑦ $1 \times 7 =$

⑧ $1 \times 8 =$

⑨ $1 \times 9 =$

⑩ $1 \times 10 =$

date / / score /100

1 Multiply.
2 points per question

① $1 \times 1 =$

② $1 \times 2 =$

③ $1 \times 3 =$

④ $1 \times 4 =$

⑤ $1 \times 5 =$

⑥ $1 \times 6 =$

⑦ $1 \times 7 =$

⑧ $1 \times 8 =$

⑨ $1 \times 9 =$

⑩ $1 \times 10 =$

2 Multiply.
2 points per question

① $1 \times 2 =$

② $1 \times 9 =$

③ $1 \times 7 =$

④ $1 \times 1 =$

⑤ $1 \times 6 =$

⑥ $1 \times 8 =$

⑦ $1 \times 10 =$

⑧ $1 \times 5 =$

⑨ $1 \times 4 =$

⑩ $1 \times 3 =$

3 Multiply.

3 points per question

① $1 \times 3 =$

② $1 \times 7 =$

③ $1 \times 1 =$

④ $1 \times 9 =$

⑤ $1 \times 5 =$

⑥ $1 \times 10 =$

⑦ $1 \times 6 =$

⑧ $1 \times 4 =$

⑨ $1 \times 7 =$

⑩ $1 \times 2 =$

⑪ $1 \times 8 =$

⑫ $1 \times 1 =$

⑬ $1 \times 10 =$

⑭ $1 \times 3 =$

⑮ $1 \times 6 =$

⑯ $1 \times 9 =$

⑰ $1 \times 5 =$

⑱ $1 \times 8 =$

⑲ $1 \times 2 =$

⑳ $1 \times 4 =$

Take a bow!

1 Multiply.

2 points per question

① $10 \times 1 =$

② $10 \times 2 =$

③ $10 \times 3 =$

④ $10 \times 4 =$

⑤ $10 \times 5 =$

⑥ $10 \times 6 =$

⑦ $10 \times 7 =$

⑧ $10 \times 8 =$

⑨ $10 \times 9 =$

⑩ $10 \times 10 =$

2 Multiply.

2 points per question

① $1 \times 1 =$

② $1 \times 2 =$

③ $1 \times 3 =$

④ $1 \times 4 =$

⑤ $1 \times 5 =$

⑥ $1 \times 6 =$

⑦ $1 \times 7 =$

⑧ $1 \times 8 =$

⑨ $1 \times 9 =$

⑩ $1 \times 10 =$

3 Multiply.

3 points per question

① 1 × 8 =

② 8 × 2 =

③ 2 × 9 =

④ 4 × 6 =

⑤ 10 × 4 =

⑥ 7 × 10 =

⑦ 3 × 7 =

⑧ 5 × 3 =

⑨ 6 × 6 =

⑩ 9 × 1 =

⑪ 7 × 8 =

⑫ 1 × 4 =

⑬ 5 × 7 =

⑭ 8 × 2 =

⑮ 9 × 5 =

⑯ 2 × 1 =

⑰ 6 × 10 =

⑱ 4 × 9 =

⑲ 10 × 3 =

⑳ 3 × 5 =

Bravo!

1 Multiply.

2 points per question

① $7 \times 7 =$

② $1 \times 6 =$

③ $5 \times 2 =$

④ $6 \times 3 =$

⑤ $9 \times 8 =$

⑥ $2 \times 4 =$

⑦ $8 \times 5 =$

⑧ $4 \times 10 =$

⑨ $10 \times 1 =$

⑩ $3 \times 9 =$

⑪ $1 \times 9 =$

⑫ $8 \times 3 =$

⑬ $2 \times 10 =$

⑭ $4 \times 7 =$

⑮ $10 \times 5 =$

⑯ $7 \times 1 =$

⑰ $3 \times 8 =$

⑱ $5 \times 4 =$

⑲ $6 \times 2 =$

⑳ $9 \times 6 =$

㉑ $6 \times 5 =$

㉒ $2 \times 1 =$

㉓ $5 \times 10 =$

㉔ $8 \times 6 =$

㉕ $4 \times 8 =$

2 Multiply.

2 points per question

① $3 \times 10 =$

② $10 \times 2 =$

③ $4 \times 1 =$

④ $8 \times 6 =$

⑤ $2 \times 5 =$

⑥ $9 \times 9 =$

⑦ $6 \times 4 =$

⑧ $5 \times 1 =$

⑨ $1 \times 7 =$

⑩ $7 \times 8 =$

⑪ $9 \times 2 =$

⑫ $6 \times 7 =$

⑬ $5 \times 5 =$

⑭ $3 \times 9 =$

⑮ $7 \times 2 =$

⑯ $10 \times 10 =$

⑰ $4 \times 8 =$

⑱ $2 \times 3 =$

⑲ $8 \times 4 =$

⑳ $1 \times 10 =$

㉑ $7 \times 9 =$

㉒ $3 \times 3 =$

㉓ $10 \times 7 =$

㉔ $9 \times 4 =$

㉕ $1 \times 2 =$

You're almost at the end.

Review:
Multiplication: 1 to 10

date   /   /   score   /100

1 Multiply.

2 points per question

① $4 \times 5 =$

② $10 \times 9 =$

③ $7 \times 3 =$

④ $3 \times 4 =$

⑤ $5 \times 6 =$

⑥ $6 \times 8 =$

⑦ $9 \times 4 =$

⑧ $1 \times 1 =$

⑨ $8 \times 8 =$

⑩ $2 \times 7 =$

⑪ $6 \times 9 =$

⑫ $9 \times 10 =$

⑬ $2 \times 6 =$

⑭ $8 \times 7 =$

⑮ $4 \times 2 =$

⑯ $10 \times 3 =$

⑰ $3 \times 1 =$

⑱ $7 \times 5 =$

⑲ $1 \times 2 =$

⑳ $5 \times 10 =$

㉑ $10 \times 6 =$

㉒ $8 \times 4 =$

㉓ $3 \times 2 =$

㉔ $1 \times 9 =$

㉕ $5 \times 7 =$

2 Multiply.

① $6 \times 10 =$

② $9 \times 3 =$

③ $2 \times 8 =$

④ $8 \times 1 =$

⑤ $4 \times 4 =$

⑥ $10 \times 7 =$

⑦ $3 \times 2 =$

⑧ $7 \times 6 =$

⑨ $1 \times 5 =$

⑩ $5 \times 9 =$

⑪ $4 \times 3 =$

⑫ $10 \times 8 =$

⑬ $7 \times 4 =$

⑭ $3 \times 6 =$

⑮ $5 \times 8 =$

⑯ $6 \times 1 =$

⑰ $2 \times 2 =$

⑱ $1 \times 3 =$

⑲ $8 \times 9 =$

⑳ $9 \times 7 =$

㉑ $4 \times 10 =$

㉒ $2 \times 5 =$

㉓ $6 \times 3 =$

㉔ $7 \times 1 =$

㉕ $9 \times 8 =$

You did it!
Congratulations!

1 Multiplication: 2 P2-3

1

①
1	2	3	4	5	6	7	8	9	10
11	12	13	14	15	16	17	18	19	20

②
2	4	6	8	10	12	14	16	18	20

③
2	4	6	8	10	12	14	16	18	20

④
2	4	6	8	10	12	14	16	18	20

2
①2　②4　③6
④8　⑤10　⑥12
⑦14　⑧16　⑨18
⑩20

3
①2　②4　③6
④8　⑤10　⑥12
⑦14　⑧16　⑨18
⑩20

4
①2　②4　③6
④8　⑤10　⑥12
⑦14　⑧16　⑨18
⑩20

2 Multiplication: 2 P4-5

1
①2　②4　③6
④8　⑤10　⑥12
⑦14　⑧16　⑨18
⑩20

2
①6　②20　③10
④4　⑤8　⑥2
⑦18　⑧14　⑨12
⑩16

3
①6　②18　③20
④2　⑤10　⑥4
⑦14　⑧8　⑨16
⑩2　⑪12　⑫6
⑬14　⑭20　⑮8
⑯12　⑰18　⑱4
⑲16　⑳10

3 Multiplication: 3 P6-7

1

①
1	2	3	4	5	6	7	8	9	10
11	12	13	14	15	16	17	18	19	20
21	22	23	24	25	26	27	28	29	30

②
3	6	9	12	15	18	21	24	27	30

③
3	6	9	12	15	18	21	24	27	30

④
3	6	9	12	15	18	21	24	27	30

2
①3　②6　③9
④12　⑤15　⑥18
⑦21　⑧24　⑨27
⑩30

3
①3　②6　③9
④12　⑤15　⑥18
⑦21　⑧24　⑨27
⑩30

4
①3　②6　③9
④12　⑤15　⑥18
⑦21　⑧24　⑨27
⑩30

4 Multiplication: 3 P8-9

1 ① 3 ② 6 ③ 9
④ 12 ⑤ 15 ⑥ 18
⑦ 21 ⑧ 24 ⑨ 27
⑩ 30

2 ① 24 ② 21 ③ 3
④ 6 ⑤ 30 ⑥ 18
⑦ 27 ⑧ 12 ⑨ 15
⑩ 9

3 ① 15 ② 24 ③ 6
④ 27 ⑤ 18 ⑥ 12
⑦ 30 ⑧ 21 ⑨ 9
⑩ 18 ⑪ 3 ⑫ 24
⑬ 12 ⑭ 21 ⑮ 6
⑯ 15 ⑰ 3 ⑱ 30
⑲ 27 ⑳ 9

5 Review: Multiplication: 2 and 3 P10-11

1 ① 2 ② 4 ③ 6
④ 8 ⑤ 10 ⑥ 12
⑦ 14 ⑧ 16 ⑨ 18
⑩ 20

2 ① 3 ② 6 ③ 9
④ 12 ⑤ 15 ⑥ 18
⑦ 21 ⑧ 24 ⑨ 27
⑩ 30

3 ① 10 ② 24 ③ 4
④ 18 ⑤ 18 ⑥ 12
⑦ 20 ⑧ 21 ⑨ 6
⑩ 12 ⑪ 3 ⑫ 16
⑬ 8 ⑭ 14 ⑮ 6
⑯ 15 ⑰ 2 ⑱ 30
⑲ 27 ⑳ 9

6 Multiplication: 4 P12-13

1

①
1	2	3	4	5	6	7	8	9	10
11	12	13	14	15	16	17	18	19	20
21	22	23	24	25	26	27	28	29	30
31	32	33	34	35	36	37	38	39	40

②
4	8	12	16	20	24	28	32	36	40

③
4	8	12	16	20	24	28	32	36	40

④
4	8	12	16	20	24	28	32	36	40

2 ① 4 ② 8 ③ 12
④ 16 ⑤ 20 ⑥ 24
⑦ 28 ⑧ 32 ⑨ 36
⑩ 40

3 ① 4 ② 8 ③ 12
④ 16 ⑤ 20 ⑥ 24
⑦ 28 ⑧ 32 ⑨ 36
⑩ 40

4 ① 4 ② 8 ③ 12
④ 16 ⑤ 20 ⑥ 24
⑦ 28 ⑧ 32 ⑨ 36
⑩ 40

7 Multiplication: 4 P14-15

1 ① 4 ② 8 ③ 12
④ 16 ⑤ 20 ⑥ 24
⑦ 28 ⑧ 32 ⑨ 36
⑩ 40

2 ① 12 ② 28 ③ 16
④ 8 ⑤ 36 ⑥ 24
⑦ 40 ⑧ 32 ⑨ 4
⑩ 20

3
① 36	② 12	③ 4
④ 40	⑤ 8	⑥ 20
⑦ 28	⑧ 16	⑨ 32
⑩ 24	⑪ 4	⑫ 28
⑬ 12	⑭ 40	⑮ 24
⑯ 16	⑰ 8	⑱ 36
⑲ 20	⑳ 32	

8 Multiplication: 5   P16-17

1

①
1	2	3	4	5	6	7	8	9	10
11	12	13	14	15	16	17	18	19	20
21	22	23	24	25	26	27	28	29	30
31	32	33	34	35	36	37	38	39	40

②
5	10	15	20	25	30	35	40	45	50

③
5	10	15	20	25	30	35	40	45	50

④
5	10	15	20	25	30	35	40	45	50

2
① 5	② 10	③ 15
④ 20	⑤ 25	⑥ 30
⑦ 35	⑧ 40	⑨ 45
⑩ 50		

3
① 5	② 10	③ 15
④ 20	⑤ 25	⑥ 30
⑦ 35	⑧ 40	⑨ 45
⑩ 50		

4
① 5	② 10	③ 15
④ 20	⑤ 25	⑥ 30
⑦ 35	⑧ 40	⑨ 45
⑩ 50		

9 Multiplication: 5   P18-19

1
① 5	② 10	③ 15
④ 20	⑤ 25	⑥ 30
⑦ 35	⑧ 40	⑨ 45
⑩ 50		

2
① 25	② 5	③ 40
④ 50	⑤ 30	⑥ 45
⑦ 10	⑧ 20	⑨ 35
⑩ 15		

3
① 40	② 25	③ 45
④ 10	⑤ 20	⑥ 30
⑦ 50	⑧ 15	⑨ 35
⑩ 5	⑪ 30	⑫ 40
⑬ 20	⑭ 35	⑮ 25
⑯ 10	⑰ 50	⑱ 5
⑲ 15	⑳ 45	

10 Review: Multiplication: 2 to 5   P20-21

1
① 4	② 8	③ 12
④ 16	⑤ 20	⑥ 24
⑦ 28	⑧ 32	⑨ 36
⑩ 40		

2
① 5	② 10	③ 15
④ 20	⑤ 25	⑥ 30
⑦ 35	⑧ 40	⑨ 45
⑩ 50		

3
① 9	② 32	③ 10
④ 15	⑤ 16	⑥ 18
⑦ 40	⑧ 35	⑨ 24
⑩ 24	⑪ 12	⑫ 40
⑬ 21	⑭ 6	⑮ 8
⑯ 20	⑰ 20	⑱ 4
⑲ 45	⑳ 12	

⑪ Multiplication: 6 P22-23

1

①
1	2	3	4	5	6	7	8	9	10
11	12	13	14	15	16	17	18	19	20
21	22	23	24	25	26	27	28	29	30
31	32	33	34	35	36	37	38	39	40

②
6	12	18	24	30	36	42	48	54	60

③
6	12	18	24	30	36	42	48	54	60

④
6	12	18	24	30	36	42	48	54	60

2
① 6 ② 12 ③ 18
④ 24 ⑤ 30 ⑥ 36
⑦ 42 ⑧ 48 ⑨ 54
⑩ 60

3
① 6 ② 12 ③ 18
④ 24 ⑤ 30 ⑥ 36
⑦ 42 ⑧ 48 ⑨ 54
⑩ 60

4
① 6 ② 12 ③ 18
④ 24 ⑤ 30 ⑥ 36
⑦ 42 ⑧ 48 ⑨ 54
⑩ 60

⑫ Multiplication: 6 P24-25

1
① 6 ② 12 ③ 18
④ 24 ⑤ 30 ⑥ 36
⑦ 42 ⑧ 48 ⑨ 54
⑩ 60

2
① 42 ② 12 ③ 36
④ 6 ⑤ 30 ⑥ 54
⑦ 24 ⑧ 48 ⑨ 18
⑩ 60

3
① 18 ② 54 ③ 6
④ 60 ⑤ 30 ⑥ 12
⑦ 24 ⑧ 42 ⑨ 36
⑩ 48 ⑪ 42 ⑫ 6
⑬ 18 ⑭ 36 ⑮ 60
⑯ 12 ⑰ 30 ⑱ 54
⑲ 24 ⑳ 48

⑬ Multiplication: 7 P26-27

1

①
1	2	3	4	5	6	7	8	9	10
11	12	13	14	15	16	17	18	19	20
21	22	23	24	25	26	27	28	29	30
31	32	33	34	35	36	37	38	39	40

②
7	14	21	28	35	42	49	56	63	70

③
7	14	21	28	35	42	49	56	63	70

④
7	14	21	28	35	42	49	56	63	70

2
① 7 ② 14 ③ 21
④ 28 ⑤ 35 ⑥ 42
⑦ 49 ⑧ 56 ⑨ 63
⑩ 70

3
① 7 ② 14 ③ 21
④ 28 ⑤ 35 ⑥ 42
⑦ 49 ⑧ 56 ⑨ 63
⑩ 70

4
① 7 ② 14 ③ 21
④ 28 ⑤ 35 ⑥ 42
⑦ 49 ⑧ 56 ⑨ 63
⑩ 70

14 Multiplication: 7 P28-29

1
① 7   ② 14   ③ 21
④ 28   ⑤ 35   ⑥ 42
⑦ 49   ⑧ 56   ⑨ 63
⑩ 70

2
① 21   ② 56   ③ 70
④ 28   ⑤ 63   ⑥ 35
⑦ 42   ⑧ 14   ⑨ 7
⑩ 49

3
① 28   ② 56   ③ 14
④ 35   ⑤ 63   ⑥ 42
⑦ 70   ⑧ 21   ⑨ 7
⑩ 56   ⑪ 49   ⑫ 14
⑬ 42   ⑭ 28   ⑮ 49
⑯ 70   ⑰ 7   ⑱ 35
⑲ 21   ⑳ 63

15 Review: Multiplication: 2 to 7 P30-31

1
① 6   ② 12   ③ 18
④ 24   ⑤ 30   ⑥ 36
⑦ 42   ⑧ 48   ⑨ 54
⑩ 60

2
① 7   ② 14   ③ 21
④ 28   ⑤ 35   ⑥ 42
⑦ 49   ⑧ 56   ⑨ 63
⑩ 70

3
① 15   ② 40   ③ 8
④ 18   ⑤ 36   ⑥ 28
⑦ 20   ⑧ 42   ⑨ 9
⑩ 30   ⑪ 7   ⑫ 32
⑬ 12   ⑭ 49   ⑮ 4
⑯ 20   ⑰ 5   ⑱ 60
⑲ 63   ⑳ 18

16 Multiplication: 8 P32-33

1

	1	2	3	4	5	6	7	8	9	10
①	11	12	13	14	15	16	17	18	19	20
	21	22	23	24	25	26	27	28	29	30
	31	32	33	34	35	36	37	38	39	40

②	8	16	24	32	40	48	56	64	72	80
③	8	16	24	32	40	48	56	64	72	80
④	8	16	24	32	40	48	56	64	72	80

2
① 8   ② 16   ③ 24
④ 32   ⑤ 40   ⑥ 48
⑦ 56   ⑧ 64   ⑨ 72
⑩ 80

3
① 8   ② 16   ③ 24
④ 32   ⑤ 40   ⑥ 48
⑦ 56   ⑧ 64   ⑨ 72
⑩ 80

4
① 8   ② 16   ③ 24
④ 32   ⑤ 40   ⑥ 48
⑦ 56   ⑧ 64   ⑨ 72
⑩ 80

17 Multiplication: 8 P34-35

1
① 8   ② 16   ③ 24
④ 32   ⑤ 40   ⑥ 48
⑦ 56   ⑧ 64   ⑨ 72
⑩ 80

2
① 56   ② 16   ③ 48
④ 8   ⑤ 72   ⑥ 40
⑦ 80   ⑧ 32   ⑨ 64
⑩ 24

3
① 24 ② 72 ③ 40
④ 8 ⑤ 80 ⑥ 56
⑦ 32 ⑧ 48 ⑨ 16
⑩ 56 ⑪ 64 ⑫ 8
⑬ 24 ⑭ 80 ⑮ 48
⑯ 72 ⑰ 40 ⑱ 16
⑲ 64 ⑳ 32

⑱ Multiplication: 9   P36-37

1

1	2	3	4	5	6	7	8	9	10
11	12	13	14	15	16	17	18	19	20
21	22	23	24	25	26	27	28	29	30
31	32	33	34	35	36	37	38	39	40

① (above grid)

② | 9 | 18 | 27 | 36 | 45 | 54 | 63 | 72 | 81 | 90 |

③ | 9 | 18 | 27 | 36 | 45 | 54 | 63 | 72 | 81 | 90 |

④ | 9 | 18 | 27 | 36 | 45 | 54 | 63 | 72 | 81 | 90 |

2
① 9 ② 18 ③ 27
④ 36 ⑤ 45 ⑥ 54
⑦ 63 ⑧ 72 ⑨ 81
⑩ 90

3
① 9 ② 18 ③ 27
④ 36 ⑤ 45 ⑥ 54
⑦ 63 ⑧ 72 ⑨ 81
⑩ 90

4
① 9 ② 18 ③ 27
④ 36 ⑤ 45 ⑥ 54
⑦ 63 ⑧ 72 ⑨ 81
⑩ 90

⑲ Multiplication: 9   P38-39

1
① 9 ② 18 ③ 27
④ 36 ⑤ 45 ⑥ 54
⑦ 63 ⑧ 72 ⑨ 81
⑩ 90

2
① 72 ② 36 ③ 90
④ 45 ⑤ 27 ⑥ 9
⑦ 54 ⑧ 18 ⑨ 63
⑩ 81

3
① 36 ② 18 ③ 72
④ 45 ⑤ 81 ⑥ 54
⑦ 27 ⑧ 90 ⑨ 9
⑩ 72 ⑪ 18 ⑫ 63
⑬ 36 ⑭ 54 ⑮ 90
⑯ 45 ⑰ 81 ⑱ 9
⑲ 63 ⑳ 27

⑳ Review: Multiplication: 2 to 9   P40-41

1
① 8 ② 16 ③ 24
④ 32 ⑤ 40 ⑥ 48
⑦ 56 ⑧ 64 ⑨ 72
⑩ 80

2
① 9 ② 18 ③ 27
④ 36 ⑤ 45 ⑥ 54
⑦ 63 ⑧ 72 ⑨ 81
⑩ 90

3
① 8 ② 72 ③ 8
④ 28 ⑤ 10 ⑥ 15
⑦ 6 ⑧ 70 ⑨ 18
⑩ 24 ⑪ 35 ⑫ 32
⑬ 18 ⑭ 27 ⑮ 30
⑯ 24 ⑰ 80 ⑱ 63
⑲ 21 ⑳ 36

21 Multiplication: 10   P42-43

1

①
1	2	3	4	5	6	7	8	9	10
11	12	13	14	15	16	17	18	19	20
21	22	23	24	25	26	27	28	29	30
31	32	33	34	35	36	37	38	39	40

②
10	20	30	40	50	60	70	80	90	100

③
10	20	30	40	50	60	70	80	90	100

④
10	20	30	40	50	60	70	80	90	100

2
① 10 ② 20 ③ 30
④ 40 ⑤ 50 ⑥ 60
⑦ 70 ⑧ 80 ⑨ 90
⑩ 100

3
① 10 ② 20 ③ 30
④ 40 ⑤ 50 ⑥ 60
⑦ 70 ⑧ 80 ⑨ 90
⑩ 100

4
① 10 ② 20 ③ 30
④ 40 ⑤ 50 ⑥ 60
⑦ 70 ⑧ 80 ⑨ 90
⑩ 100

22 Multiplication: 10   P44-45

1
① 10 ② 20 ③ 30
④ 40 ⑤ 50 ⑥ 60
⑦ 70 ⑧ 80 ⑨ 90
⑩ 100

2
① 90 ② 70 ③ 20
④ 60 ⑤ 10 ⑥ 30
⑦ 50 ⑧ 100 ⑨ 40
⑩ 80

3
① 80 ② 10 ③ 100
④ 30 ⑤ 60 ⑥ 90
⑦ 50 ⑧ 80 ⑨ 20
⑩ 40 ⑪ 30 ⑫ 70
⑬ 10 ⑭ 90 ⑮ 50
⑯ 100 ⑰ 60 ⑱ 40
⑲ 70 ⑳ 20

23 Multiplication: 1   P46-47

1

①
1	2	3	4	5	6	7	8	9	10

②
1	2	3	4	5	6	7	8	9	10

③
1	2	3	4	5	6	7	8	9	10

④
1	2	3	4	5	6	7	8	9	10

2
① 1 ② 2 ③ 3
④ 4 ⑤ 5 ⑥ 6
⑦ 7 ⑧ 8 ⑨ 9
⑩ 10

3
① 1 ② 2 ③ 3
④ 4 ⑤ 5 ⑥ 6
⑦ 7 ⑧ 8 ⑨ 9
⑩ 10

4
① 1 ② 2 ③ 3
④ 4 ⑤ 5 ⑥ 6
⑦ 7 ⑧ 8 ⑨ 9
⑩ 10

24 Multiplication: 1   P48-49

1
① 1 ② 2 ③ 3
④ 4 ⑤ 5 ⑥ 6
⑦ 7 ⑧ 8 ⑨ 9
⑩ 10

2
① 2 ② 9 ③ 7
④ 1 ⑤ 6 ⑥ 8
⑦ 10 ⑧ 5 ⑨ 4
⑩ 3

3
① 3 ② 7 ③ 1
④ 9 ⑤ 5 ⑥ 10
⑦ 6 ⑧ 4 ⑨ 7
⑩ 2 ⑪ 8 ⑫ 1
⑬ 10 ⑭ 3 ⑮ 6
⑯ 9 ⑰ 5 ⑱ 8
⑲ 2 ⑳ 4

25 Review: Multiplication: 1 to 10

1
① 10 ② 20 ③ 30
④ 40 ⑤ 50 ⑥ 60
⑦ 70 ⑧ 80 ⑨ 90
⑩ 100

2
① 1 ② 2 ③ 3
④ 4 ⑤ 5 ⑥ 6
⑦ 7 ⑧ 8 ⑨ 9
⑩ 10

3
① 8 ② 16 ③ 18
④ 24 ⑤ 40 ⑥ 70
⑦ 21 ⑧ 15 ⑨ 36
⑩ 9 ⑪ 56 ⑫ 4
⑬ 35 ⑭ 16 ⑮ 45
⑯ 2 ⑰ 60 ⑱ 36
⑲ 30 ⑳ 15

26 Review: Multiplication: 1 to 10
P52-53

1
① 49 ② 6 ③ 10
④ 18 ⑤ 72 ⑥ 8
⑦ 40 ⑧ 40 ⑨ 10
⑩ 27 ⑪ 9 ⑫ 24
⑬ 20 ⑭ 28 ⑮ 50
⑯ 7 ⑰ 24 ⑱ 20
⑲ 12 ⑳ 54 ㉑ 30
㉒ 2 ㉓ 50 ㉔ 48
㉕ 32

2
① 30 ② 20 ③ 4
④ 48 ⑤ 10 ⑥ 81
⑦ 24 ⑧ 5 ⑨ 7
⑩ 56 ⑪ 18 ⑫ 42
⑬ 25 ⑭ 27 ⑮ 14
⑯ 100 ⑰ 32 ⑱ 6
⑲ 32 ⑳ 10 ㉑ 63
㉒ 9 ㉓ 70 ㉔ 36
㉕ 2

27 Review: Multiplication: 1 to 10
P54-55

1
① 20 ② 90 ③ 21
④ 12 ⑤ 30 ⑥ 48
⑦ 36 ⑧ 1 ⑨ 64
⑩ 14 ⑪ 54 ⑫ 90
⑬ 12 ⑭ 56 ⑮ 8
⑯ 30 ⑰ 3 ⑱ 35
⑲ 2 ⑳ 50 ㉑ 60
㉒ 32 ㉓ 6 ㉔ 9
㉕ 35

2 ① 60   ② 27   ③ 16
④ 8   ⑤ 16   ⑥ 70
⑦ 6   ⑧ 42   ⑨ 5
⑩ 45   ⑪ 12   ⑫ 80
⑬ 28   ⑭ 18   ⑮ 40
⑯ 6   ⑰ 4   ⑱ 3
⑲ 72   ⑳ 63   ㉑ 40
㉒ 10   ㉓ 18   ㉔ 7
㉕ 72